HAMZAT'S JOURNEY

A Refugee Diary

Anthony Robinson

Series Editor

Annemarie Young

Illustrated by June Allan

This is Hamzat's own story. It's the story of how his life, and that of his family, changed forever on 20 April, 2001. That was the day he stepped on a landmine while on his way to school with two friends. It is the story of his journey from Grozny, in Chechnya, to Magas in Ingushetia, on to Vladicaucasus in North Ossetia and finally to Baku in Azerbaijan where he waited for the plane to take him to England . . . and a new life.

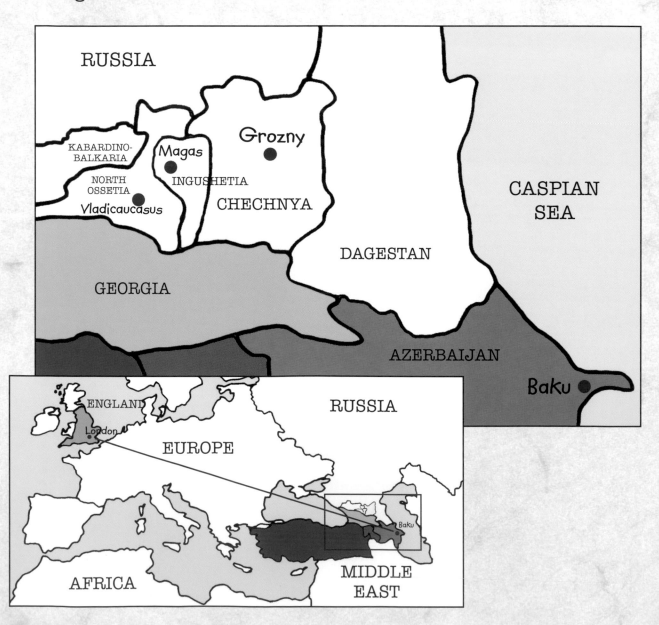

This is a picture of me

My name is Hamzat. I was born in Grozny, Chechnya, in 1993. This was during our war with Russia. My mum says I was born with a bang. I have an older brother, Zaurbek, who is 17, and a little sister, Kheda, who is seven. My mum's name is Tamara and my dad is called Zelim.

This is my story and it's about how, in a funny way, being unlucky has been lucky in the end for me and my whole family.

Early days – Grozny, 1993-2000

The war between the Chechen fighters and the Russians had been going on since 1991. My dad has told me a lot about this and why people were fighting the Russians. I don't really understand it. All I remember of that time is war. It was just better or worse war, but always war. We were always hungry, afraid and cold in winter. Very, very cold. We still went to school and I liked that and being with my friends. Our school had been bombed, but we had lessons OK in the shell of the school buildings.

Bomb-damaged buildings in Chechnya

That was my life. You just got used to it. My mum and dad said it was hard. There was no electricity or gas after the 1994-95 Russian bombings. Even the sewers were all blocked up. I remember when I was five going down to a spring to get water early in the morning and carrying a two-litre drum back. It was heavy. We were hiding in a basement in those days and it was cold and dark, and scary at night with the bombings. Mornings were OK as they mostly bombed at night.

Life goes on – Grozny 1993–2000

So, apart from the trouble all around us, we were just
a family. We did normal stuff. I went to school, we ate
and talked like any family, but the trouble was all around us.
The noise of explosions, the broken buildings. You couldn't
ignore it, but you had to.

My little sister in the snow

I still remember my little sister used to cry 'Where's mummy gone?' when Mum was outside trying to cook on a fire or getting water. Dad was an engineer before all the trouble, but then there was no work. Sometimes he did building repair work, but that's all.

After the Russians took over Grozny, in the winter of 2000, it got worse even though the fighting was over. The soldiers would come every day to check the houses for fighters and weapons. Sometimes they would come in the middle of the night. You could be just sleeping and suddenly, 'bang, bang' on the door.
We were all scared then.
Cold, hungry and
scared.

That step – Friday, 20 April, 2001

Then it happened. On a normal day, walking to school, like I always did, with my friends.

I stepped on a landmine.

I don't remember the explosion. I was unconscious some of the time and sometimes awake. I just don't remember all that much. I later found out that a passer-by took me to hospital in his car. I think I got that car really dirty. I'm sorry for that. He was kind. I do remember one thing. He kept asking me my name. He put a belt around my shattered leg, for the bleeding, I suppose.

I don't remember when I realised that I had lost my
right foot. People didn't want to tell me, I think, but I knew.
I remember too, that I could still feel my foot, even though
it wasn't there.

Someone must have told my parents because my mum
came pretty soon. My dad couldn't because the roads were
blocked by the Russians. I had the operation that day.

Hospital and the operation –
20-21 April, 2001

I don't remember much about the operation. They gave me
an injection, then I heard them putting on rubber gloves . . .
and then I was off. I was completely numbed out.

My leg and foot were amputated below the knee because
the bones were so shattered. The doctor who operated on me
was called Salman Yandarov, a famous Chechnyan surgeon.
We had to pay for it and Grandma could afford it. I was lucky,
I suppose.

I kept asking about the other kids who were with me, because I couldn't see them in the hospital. I only learned later, after I got home, that they had been killed that day.

I had to have a blood transfusion on the second day because I was getting too weak. My dad gave most of the blood. And it was a funny thing. The foot I didn't have any more was really itchy.

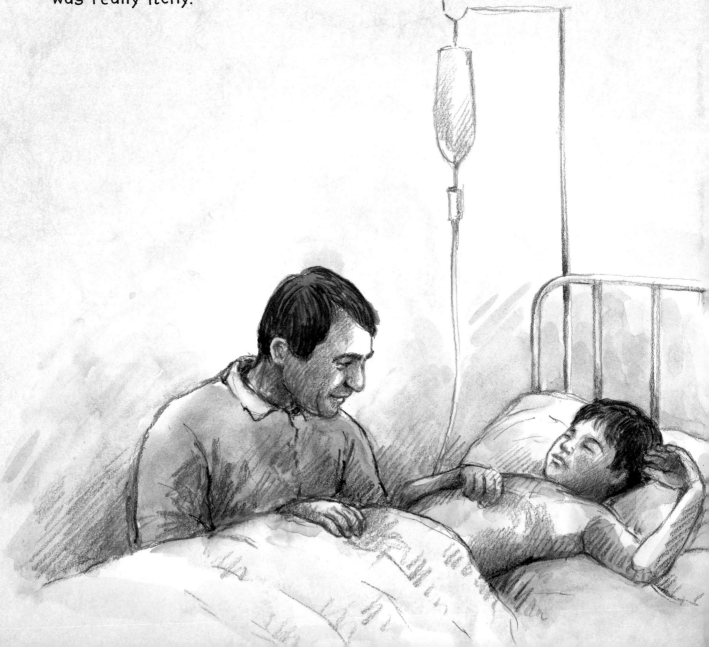

Getting better – 21 April – 6 May, 2001

The Russians bombed the hospital while I was there.
It was May Day, a special day in Russian history, so
the Russian soldiers were celebrating.

Mum visited me every day in hospital. I was quite
embarrassed to be in a women's ward, but I had no
choice because the men's ward was full. I wasn't hungry
in the beginning but after a couple of days they gave
me some kind of injections, then I was really hungry.
Mum kept bringing me food. I put on some weight then.
I wasn't so skinny any more.

Then I got an infection in my wounds. They had to open
a bit of the stitching and clean the wound. I still have a
strange, round scar where that happened. But it was OK
then, though it all seemed so slow. Hospital was boring.
It was always the same. My mum and dad came, which was
great, but it wasn't like being at home. I wanted to get
home. And I really didn't like being in there with all the
women. It was embarrassing sometimes.

I just wanted to go home.

After a week I started to use crutches because my leg
didn't hurt so much. I got used to them fairly quickly and
after 20 days of practice I left hospital to a wonderful green
spring. It was nice to be with my family and friends again.

Home at last –
Summer–Autumn, 2001

Once, my whole class came to visit, along with the head teacher. I sat on a windowsill and we just talked. It was great to *see* everybody again. Everybody except the two friends I was with the day it happened. That was hard. I just wanted to *see* them.

I didn't go out for half a month or so. Then the summer holidays started. That was good. I had time to get strong and really practise on my crutches. I got really good with them. But I wanted an artificial leg. I knew that would be better. Then, in the autumn of 2001, my parents arranged for me to get an artificial leg. I was so excited. I went with Mum on the bus to Magas, the capital of Ingushetia, which is next to Chechnya. Then UNICEF (United Nations Children's Fund) took us by car to Vladicaucasus in North Ossetia, for an artificial leg to be fitted.

Two legs are better than one –
September, 2001

We went to Magas three times. It was a long, hard bus
journey, three days there and back, but I enjoyed getting
out. It was about starting again for me. Two legged.
The first visit was for measuring me up for the leg,
the others were for fitting and getting used to it. I had
a belt round my waist to hold it up. It was hopeless.
Uncomfortable. They finally adjusted it so it was more
comfortable. I never really liked that leg, but it was
the one I had so what could I do?

Me and my new leg

In the September I went back to school and started Year 2.
It was really good to see my teacher and my friends.
I remember the English teacher wasn't very good at English,
but it was a start for me, so when I came here to England
it wasn't all completely strange.

A new life –
October–November, 2001

At about this time an organisation called Ccharm (Children of Chechnya Action Relief Mission) got in touch with my family. They are a charity that helps children badly injured by war. They wanted to help us get to England where they could fit a really good artificial leg. So, on 9 November, 2001, me and Dad went back to Ingushetia to meet people from Ccharm. Another boy was also there. His name was Islam and he had lost both eyes and both arms. He was there with his brother, Musa.

Carlo di Pamparato, Islam and me

We then went to Baku in Azerbaijan, where we waited for five days in a hotel for the man who was going to help us with documents, Carlo di Pamparato from Ccharm. Then it all happened, and before I knew it I was on a plane headed for England. It was my first time in a plane. It was great.

Arriving in England –
November 2001–April 2002

We arrived at Heathrow airport on 16 November, 2001.
We had all the papers we needed for a six-month stay
for treatment in the UK. Carlo rented a flat for us for
three months on Edgware Road in London. During that
time Islam and I had treatment in a hospital, North
something. I've forgotten where exactly, but a car would
come and take us there. I got a new, better leg and
Islam got arms. After the three months were up, we
went to live in a flat belonging to a Chechen, in Seven
Sisters, in London. We were still all together. It was OK.

Me and my new leg

What happened next came as a complete surprise to me.
But my dad must have been planning it for some time,
because on 16 April, 2002, we went to the Home Office
in Croydon and applied for asylum.

I was a bit upset about maybe never going home again
and not seeing my mum and stuff. I don't know what
happened to Islam and his brother. We moved again then,
into another flat, and they went off somewhere else.

I spent loads of time learning English then. We were just
waiting. A journalist I had met gave us some books and a
dictionary and we had a Chechen interpreter who helped me
a lot with my English. He was really kind.

Our new life –
April 2002–Summer 2007

On 1 December, 2004, we were granted refugee status.
As soon as that happened my Dad just said, 'We're
going to get the rest of the family over here too now'.
Just like that. I was really excited about that. And on
26 March, 2005, they arrived at Luton airport. Dad says
we have a lot to thank Ccharm for.

Me and Dad in Trafalgar Square

Mum says Dad applied for the rest of the family to come because he doesn't like cooking!

Life then got normal for us. I started school in September, 2005 at Woodbury Down Primary School. I went into year 5 and I was 11. This was a year behind for my age, but six months later they moved me into Year 6, even before the SATS. I was glad. I really loved being there. It had a huge playground, which was great for us to run around in.

I didn't have any special English lessons. I don't know how I've learned it really. Just picked it up in bits and bobs. I think TV was my main teacher. We also have a Chechen friend who speaks English, and I ask him all sorts of questions.

The Future

My high school is Bow School. It's a boy's only school. Everybody round here just calls it Bow Boys. I was a bit worried at first about losing my friends when I moved into high school, but lots of my friends are at Bow anyway.

I like school a lot. But I suppose I like Technology, Science and Art the best. Out of school, I really enjoy basketball, reading graphic comics and playing computer games with friends.

And the further future . . . I just don't know. Mum went home for a month last summer and says everything back in Grozny is stable. New buildings are going up and the fighting has stopped. I am hoping to go back for a visit with the rest of the family next summer. So, we'll see. I am happy here. My life is settled, I have friends and a good school, but sometimes I think it would be good to go home. If I go back in the summer, it will be easier to make up my mind. Maybe.

Did you Know?

★ Chechnya is a Republic within the Russian Federation. It is located on the northern slopes of the Caucasus Mountains, just 100 kilometres (60 miles) from the Caspian Sea. It is surrounded on nearly all sides by territories in the Russian Federation: Stavropol Krai in the north west, Dagestan to the north east and east, Ingushetia and North Ossetia to the west. Georgia, which is not in the Russian Federation, is on its southern border.

★ It covers an area of about 15,500 square kilometres (just under 10,000 square miles).

★ The capital city is Grozny.

★ The three main rivers are the Sunzha, Terek and the Argun.

★ The population is a little over one million people and they speak Chechen and Russian.

★ The people of the Caucasus have fought against foreign control since Turkish occupation in the 15th century. They continue to struggle to this day against Russian control, which was first established two centuries ago.

What happened?

The history of Chechnya is a long and troubled one. This is just a brief outline.

Russia has held Chechnya with a strong hand since it was absorbed into the Russian Empire in the 19th century. Since that time there has been ongoing trouble, with Christian groups opposed to Muslim groups, and rebels fighting against Russian control.

Significant deposits of oil were discovered in the late 19th century and the railway was established. This brought with it a time of stability and some prosperity, until the Second World War. There was then a very difficult period, which lasted until 1957.

The current problems started in the early 1990s and led to the First and Second Chechen Wars. The First War started after the Chechen Parliament declared independence from Russia in 1991, and armed groups fought for control. In 1994, the Russian army invaded, and overran Grozny. Russia finally withdrew, largely defeated, in 1996.

Things rumbled on until 1999, when Russian troops again entered Chechnya to bring order as rival groups inside the country fought for power. Fierce fighting continued until Russia declared the end of hostilities in 2002, but internal struggles continue.

These two wars have left millions of people living in poverty, half a million refugees and most of the infrastructure (roads, hospitals, schools, water and power) destroyed. Northern Chechnya and Grozny are currently being rebuilt.

First published in Great Britain in 2009 and in the USA in 2010 by
Frances Lincoln Children's Books, 4 Torriano Mews,
Torriano Avenue, London NW5 2RZ

www.franceslincoln.com

British Library Cataloguing in Publication Data
available on request

ISBN 978-1-84780-030-5

Illustrated with watercolour

Printed in China

1 3 5 7 9 8 6 4 2